# Laugh Hyena

### Written and illustrated
### by Shoo Rayner

Laughing Hyena loved to laugh.

He loved to play tricks
on his friends, and he laughed
when he tricked them.

One day Hyena looked up at the sky.
"Look up there!" he shouted
to his friends.
"We can't see anything," they said.

"Hee, hee, hee!" said Hyena. "That's because there's nothing to see. I tricked you, and you fell for it!"

"Ha, ha, ha!" said his friends. "Very funny!"

Hyena stuck some money to the path.

Elephant was out walking.
He looked down and saw the money.
He tried and tried to pick it up,
but he couldn't.

"Hee, hee, hee!" said Hyena.
"I stuck the money to the path.
I tricked you, and you fell for it!"

"Ha, ha, ha!" said Elephant.
"Very funny!"

Hyena saw two bears digging a hole. When the bears stopped for a rest, Hyena looked into the hole.

"Oh, no!" shouted Hyena.
"You've broken a water pipe.
This hole is full of water!"

The bears ran to the hole.
They looked and they looked again.
"We can't see any water," they said.

"Hee, hee, hee!" said Hyena.
"There isn't any water.
I tricked you, and you fell for it!"

"Ha, ha, ha!" said the bears.
"Very funny!"

Hyena looked up at the sky again.
"Look up there!" he shouted.

This time his friends didn't look up.
They knew it was a trick.

Hyena stepped back.
He looked up at the sky again.
"Up there. Look!" he said.

"Don't step back, Hyena!" shouted one of the bears.

Hyena laughed. "I'm not falling for that old trick."

He stepped back again.
Down he fell into the hole. *Crash!*

"Hee, hee, hee!" said all his friends.

"Ha, ha, ha! Very funny!" said the Laughing Hyena. "I really fell for that one!"